I found this study on Me. takes an in-depth look at Scripture, with examples to apply to our own lives so we too can reach out to others. The author's heart for mentoring and touching lives will inspire you in this wonderful study.

Janice Sitzes, Director of Franklin County Baptist Women's
Ministry of Missouri

What a necessary subject — MENTORING!!! All Christian women need to have a mentor and be a mentor. Kristi Neace has written a Bible Study that will enhance the life of Christian women anywhere. It is great to see Kristi take seriously this ministry of MENTORING!!!

Vivian McCaughan
Missouri Baptist Convention
WMU/Women's Missions and Ministry

Between Friends...

A Woman's Look at Mentoring God's Way

Kristi Neace

To order more copies
of *Between Friends*
See page 87

Or contact:
CrossHouse Publishing
P.O. Box 461592
Garland, TX 75046

CALL: 1-877-212-0933
Fax: 1-888-252-3022
Email: crosshousepublishing@earthlink.net
Visit: www.crosshousebooks.com
www.crosshousepublishing.org

Unless otherwise noted, all Scripture quotations are take from Holy
Bible, New International Version, copyright 1973, 1978, 1984 by
International Bible Society
Library of Congress Control Number: 2006939062
ISBN 0-929292-39-1

Table of Contents

Foreword

The word *mentor* means a wise and trusted counselor or teacher. In the Holy Spirit, God our Father blesses His children with a wise and trusted counselor and teacher beyond compare. As God grows us in the grace and knowledge of the Lord Jesus Christ, He does not want us to keep the blessings to ourselves but to share His blessings with others. Kristi's Bible study, *Between Friends: A Woman's Look at Mentoring God's Way*, reminds us of both the privilege and responsibility we have as Christians to disciple and mentor others. May Paul's love letter to the Philippian Christians challenge each of us: "Whatever you have learned or received or heard from me, or seen in me - put into practice. And the God of peace will be with you." (Phil. 4:9)

Greg Cross, Senior Pastor
First Baptist Church
Union, MO

Preface

If you are like me, you've probably heard the phrase *Titus II woman*, but have wondered what exactly is a *Titus II woman*? The Bible describes her as a woman who is reverent in her daily life, not slandering, or addicted to wine, a teacher and a mentor to younger women, busy with everyday raising of children and the upkeep of a marriage. She should be self-controlled and pure, busy at home, kind, and subject to her husband. (Paraphrase — Titus 2:3-5)

Many of these characteristics and more will be opened to you as we explore the wide opportunities for this lady of grace and honor. Is God calling you to this special position within His body of believers? The answer is definitely YES! Dear sister, welcome to this journey and may God richly bless you along the way. I hope you will find it as fascinating as I have!

Dedication

Rick, eighteen years ago if someone would have told us that I would write a Bible study and you would be training for a marathon, we would have laughed our heads off! Glory and praise be to God that He saw us through so many of the rough spots and brought us to dependence on Him in every area of our lives. Thank you for your many years of support and love. You are my very best friend and I praise our Heavenly Father for sending you my way.

Chris, Cameron and Meghan, you have always been my rays of sunshine. I love you and pray that you will focus on Jesus and trust Him with your lives. He will never lead you astray and will bring a joy and peace that can only come through Him.

Dad and Mom, you have made such an impact on me. Your love and support have always been there, even when I didn't deserve it. I am so thankful that you raised me in a Christian home and gave me a life full of love and encouragement.

To all my family, friends, co-workers and brothers and sisters in Christ, I love you all and cherish every conversation, fun time, encouragement and blessing you have shared with me. You will never know how much you have meant to me throughout the years.

Last, but not least, to Shawn Brown, a friend for a season who encouraged and challenged me to deepen my walk with the Lord. You were a definite answer to prayer at that time in my life. May God richly bless you in all that you do.

You Called Me Friend

By Kristi Neace

I was alone but through my tears,
God heard my cries throughout those years.
Through loneliness He had a plan,
To bring you here and help me stand.
I needed a smile, a warm embrace,
anything I cried, would help me face
this longing for a friend to share
the burdens of my every care.
He brought me you, a woman like me
To encourage me on selflessly
And help me fly to victory through a
Relationship with Him.

You called me friend and helped me stand
You showed me kindness and He began
The mending of my broken heart.
You taught me things that I should know,
And through friendship God caused me to grow
And depend on Him for every need,
In every season and every deed.

Though miles or circumstance may cause us to part
Please know that you touched my heart
Because you called me friend.

Week 1

God Doesn't Call the Qualified...
He Qualifies the Called

I am so very excited to be taking this journey with you. My wonderful Savior has laid on my heart the need for a strong women's ministry and mentoring unit within our local churches. On any given Sunday, if you were to observe the congregation in which you attend, you might notice the many women who seem alone— just waiting for that kind word or loving touch of a friend. Maybe *you* are that woman. It may be that you have yearned for that sense of belonging to something or someone, yet somehow felt so disconnected. It truly breaks my heart when I see women out of touch with the very ones we are supposed to be in close fellowship with. Whether they are young or old, middle-aged or teen-aged, wealthy, or poor, uneducated or scholarly, the truth is that all women need Jesus and a support system to which they can connect with and be accountable to. Thus the design of this study.

Dear sisters, let's join together now and pray a prayer of dedication as we begin this journey, that God will protect and overshadow any thought, feeling, or doubt we may have, and that He will be glorified in and through this study and ultimately bring us to a better understanding of who He is, and what He has called us to be within the body of Christ.

Take a few moments to write a simple prayer of dedication to God for this study:

_____

_____

_____

_____

_____

_____

_____

_____

_____

_____

_____

_____

Day 1

Mentoring. We've all heard that word, but what does it really mean? As I've gotten more and more involved in women's ministry, I have found that Christian women of all ages have a purpose and role in the church. The older women have experienced things that most of us younger women have not fully encountered yet. Most of these "older girls" have walked the halls late at night with fussy babies, waited anxiously by the bedside of sick children, and prayed feverishly by the windows of their homes waiting for carefree teenagers to arrive safely. They have struggled through the early years of marriage and have learned to balance obedience to God and the needs of a growing family. Younger women, on the other hand, have acquired the stamina and exuberance that may have waned in the latter years of a middle-aged woman's life. The younger woman finds more desire to connect and build lasting friendships. Yet, she needs the guidance and encouragement of someone who has walked in her shoes and understands the frustrations and trials she may be facing.

Has anyone besides me ever cried out, "I need some help here, Lord, and I need it now!?" That is exactly what mentoring is. It is that helping hand that is quick to act with godly guidance and love, yet being honest enough to lay bear those things which need a little more "Son" exposure! Mentoring, though, doesn't have to be only between older and younger women in women's ministry. It can certainly take on many forms within a church body such as younger women mentoring teen girls, older women with younger women, and/or spiritually mature women giving godly biblical counsel to those who are weaker or new to the faith.

I have heard it said that those trained to spot counterfeit monies are grilled and drilled on the real thing. That is exactly how we are going to begin this study on mentoring, by looking at the real thing in action, then applying the truths we learn to our own lives.

Let's begin our journey in the Old Testament.

Read Ruth 1:1-22. What was the situation surrounding this family and what brought the two women (Ruth and Naomi) together and totally dependent on God and one another?

_____

_____

_____

_____

First, let's grasp the history behind this family. Elimelech, whose very name means "(My) God is King", his wife Naomi "the sweet one", and their two sons Mahlon and Kilion "sick" and "pining", were citizens of Bethlehem. There came a famine in the land, so they traveled to the land of the Moabites in order to survive. It is here, that their sons married Moabite women, Ruth and Orpah, but not before Elimelech died and Naomi was left a widow.

Just as a little mental tidbit, look back with me to Genesis 19:37. From who did the Moabite people originate?

_____

I know this may seem a little off our subject, but follow along and absorb this whole concept.

You will notice that the Moabite people came from an incestuous relationship between Lot and his elder daughter after Sodom and Gomorrah were destroyed and Lot's wife was turned into a pillar of salt. Lot's daughters saw no other way to carry on the bloodline, so they took it upon themselves to conceive through their father. The eldest daughter became pregnant and bore a son she named Moab. The Moabites became bitter enemies of Abraham's ancestors, the chosen people of Israel. During the time that Elimelech and his family traveled to Moab, there was a temporary time of peace between these two clans of people. Whew!

Okay, girls, I know we've taken a side road, but you will see how this all fits together in a minute. As you read in verses 1-12 in Ruth, you noticed that Naomi was widowed but taken care of by her two sons. Then the unthinkable happened. Her beloved sons died. Naomi's protection, provision, and promise of heirs had all but been abolished. She had no choice but to return home to whence she came. Reports were flooding back that "Jehovah Jirah" (the Lord will provide) had come to the aid of his people and had provided food. Can you imagine with me just a moment the emotion that was running around in that household? Naomi was not a spring chicken any more and being a widow meant that she depended on the care of her sons in order to survive. Now, her sons were gone as well. It had been ten long years since she had been forced to settle in the land of the Moabites, surrounded by pagan gods and idol worship. I'm sure she had left family and friends behind in Bethlehem and was longing to be back with them. More importantly, don't you just imagine that she was questioning God...the true God whom she had worshiped all these years. Why on earth would he have moved them from an empty land to a pagan land, allowed her to lose her only means of support and true family, and then back to a land of plenty? Meanwhile, her daughters-in-law were grieving for the husbands of their youth. No children had been born, and now they were left empty-handed and broken-hearted. Heirs meant everything, and now there were none.

Here is where the rubber meets the road when it comes to our topic of mentoring. Ruth, a Moabitess, and as we learned earlier from a clan who had been bitter enemies with the very people Naomi came from, shows total dedication towards Naomi. Go ahead and look with me at the following question and then we will discuss it.

What was Ruth's action towards Naomi in verse 14?

_____

_____

_____

_____

_____

_____

In this passage, we see the Hebrew word "dābaq" which refers to "loyalty, affection, to adhere to." Ruth was willing to turn away and leave everything she had ever known, including her pagan religion, in order to honor and be in the presence of her mother-in-law. Can you imagine the relationship Ruth and Naomi had developed over the tumultuous years previous? Wow! Think about it…two women from totally different backgrounds and different generations being brought together through "God-arranged" circumstances. Praise God!

Let's turn to another passage and see almost the same desperation.

Read John 13:36-38. How did Peter respond to Jesus' news of his soon departure?

_____

_____

_____

_____

I want to stop here for today so that we can digest what we've consumed and prepare for tomorrow's lesson. Before we go though, **have you ever encountered someone in your life that you respected so much to the point of clinging to them (maybe not physically, but emotionally)? If so, describe what made them so special and what characteristics they had that you would like to apply to your own life.**

_____

_____

_____

_____

_____

_____

_____

_____

_____

See you tomorrow!

Day 2

Yesterday we got our feet wet in mentoring by following the story of two very special women. Let's continue on with their examples and find out how we can apply this story to our own relationships.

Naomi realized the situation she was in. She too had been displaced from her family and her God. She wasn't about to demand these women follow her all the way back to Bethlehem. Their lives were there in Moab and had always been there. But, yet, we see that one of them, Ruth, had literally "clung" to Naomi. In verse 18 it says that *"When Naomi realized that Ruth was determined to go with her, she stopped urging her."*

Ruth had developed a love and respect for the old woman and I'm sure that Naomi as well had grown fond of Ruth. Separation at this point was a mute point. Their relationship had become as close as mother and daughter. Naomi had become Ruth's mentor, teaching her the ropes of married life and showing her how to provide a home for her husband. I think we can all imagine the hours of conversation they might have had while waiting on the bread to bake or scrubbing the clothes in their courtyard near the community well. Naomi probably shared endless tales of her first years with Elimelech, but more importantly, though, it is obvious that she shared her love and passion for her God. Ruth and Orpah probably sat wide-eyed as she recanted the old tales of how Yahweh had provided for Elimelech's forefathers and had seen her through many trials that she had faced over the years. Now that neither

Naomi nor her daughter-in-law had homes and husbands to care for, they clung to one another, building bonds that would grow stronger with time.

Proceed on through chapter 2. What are some characteristics you see of both women which made this mentor/mentee relationship flourish?

_____

_____

_____

_____

_____

_____

*Hint – see vs. 2-3; 11-12; 18-19; 22-23; 3:1; 5

Naomi and Ruth became dependent on one another. As they left Moab together, they were entering Bethlehem at harvest time. Harvest or "therismos" was a time to reap…a time followed by festivities. These two women, unbeknownst to them, were about to enter God's miraculous blessings with not only the blessings of a marriage and the birth of a child, but also the benefits of a strong friendship.

Ladies, a mentor/mentee friendship can be such a blessing! As I hope you picked up on throughout our read of Ruth, there were many characteristics that enabled this relationship to develop and thrive. First of all, there was a deep attachment and love for one another. This probably didn't happen immediately. As we women know, in most cases it takes time for us to warm up to another human being. We often put up a safety net so as not to allow too much of our inner self be exposed. This is especially true if we have been deeply hurt or traumatized. It is then that we try all the more to protect our thoughts and emotions, sparingly releasing them to another.

I have always found it quite humorous to observe a group of women who have just met each other for the first time. There are all the familiar nicety-nice comments, compliments and ooze! Let's just face it…we are all very surface until and unless we allow God to open us up and expose our inner selves. I'm sure it took several years for Ruth and Naomi to build the bond that we see in chapter one, but as we dig deeper, we also notice things such as loyalty, kindness, generosity, provision, encouragement, protection, guidance and trust. These are definitely true markings of a thriving mentor/mentee relationship.

Having said all that, let's end our session today by looking back to Galatians 5:22 and remind ourselves of some of the characteristics we are to have as godly women/Christians. Write them here.

_____

_____

_____

_____

These characteristics will not only insure the success of a mentoring relationship, but will honor God and bring glory to Him in all relationships! Let's pray for the Holy Spirit to begin a good work in us right now!

Day 3

Welcome back! It is my sincere hope and prayer that God is speaking to you somehow through this study. Let's begin our session today by taking a peek at another example of a mentor/mentee relationship.

Turn with me to Luke 1:39-56. Who were the two women in this account and what circumstances brought them together?

_____

_____

_____

_____

_____

_____

_____

_____

Have you ever had a bit of good news that you could hardly wait to tell? Maybe you were just busting at the seams with excitement, so you got on the phone and called your mom. Maybe you just hopped in the car and went to tell a friend. Whatever it was, it was something to be shared. This is exactly what we see with Mary. The angel Gabriel had just been to visit her with the shocking, yet exciting news that she had been chosen to be the vessel to bring forth God's son, the God man, Jesus Christ!

Look at vs. 39 and note the two things that describe exactly what she did.

_____

_____

_____

_____

_____

_____

_____

_____

Mary got ready and hurried! She could not wait to tell Elizabeth, a woman who would understand the news. Now I must note that this little jaunt was not down the street a few blocks. Mary's trip to Elizabeth's home probably would have taken her several days! We can only imagine how she rehearsed over and over in her mind exactly what she would say to Elizabeth and how she would explain every detail of the angel's visit. Unbelievable!

After the long, hot travel, the Holy Spirit initiated the conversation between the two women by causing the unborn John to leap in his mother's womb. This whole exciting event makes me wonder what kind of conversations took place in Zachariah's house over the next three months. We know from scripture that Mary was a young girl and Elizabeth was an old woman, yet they each had been chosen to fulfill God's plan in a miraculous way. There would ultimately be two new lives, one of which would serve the other.

If you have experienced a pregnancy, did you compare notes, so to speak, with other women who had gone through it before? If so, how did it help you to share?

_____

_____

_____

_____

_____

_____

_____

_____

_____

As we can only imagine, Elizabeth probably shared with Mary how for five long months, she had stayed in seclusion after realizing that God's promise had come true in her. She had only just recently announced the happy blessing to friends and family. She and Mary now had something in common besides blood kinship.

Imagine with me all the questions Mary had about changes that would take place in her body and how the family, and especially Joseph, would react to her secret? The two women probably spent hours talking and weaving cloth for tiny blankets to wrap their little wriggling miracles in; the younger learning from the older, yet both of them learning at the same time.

Girls, we are going to stop here for the day, but go ahead and read Mary's song of praise in verses 46-55, and write a prayer to God for the ways he has blessed you.

_____

_____

_____

_____

_____

_____

_____

_____

_____

_____

_____

_____

_____

_____

_____

_____

Day 4

As we caught a glimpse of Mary and Elizabeth yesterday and imagined the type of mentoring that took place over the three months they shared together, today we want to look at another mentoring duo, Paul and Timothy.

Like Mary and Elizabeth, we see a considerable age difference between these two men, but yet both of them were birthing the gospel and enduring many hardships and obstacles along the way together.

Read 1 Corinthians 4:17. How does Paul describe his feelings for Timothy?

_____

_____

_____

_____

_____

Have you ever wondered what it would be like to walk and talk with the apostle Paul for even five minutes? Wow! After Jesus, himself, when I get to heaven, I want to find Paul and ask him a few things. One of the main questions will definitely be: "Did you write the book of Hebrews?" It's killing me!

Timothy no doubt had many occasions to sit and talk with Paul. God has been gracious enough to give us a few glimpses of some of the counsel Paul offered to his young protégé. Join with me as we take a look.

**Read the following passages and name some of the things Paul warns his young mentee about.
(1 Timothy 4:7-8 and 12-16)**

_____

_____

_____

_____

_____

_____

What are some characteristics Paul encourages Timothy to have? (1 Timothy 6:11)

_____

_____

_____

_____

_____

_____

As we end today's lesson, be reminded of someone who has had a profound influence on your life. Maybe you haven't had that guidance and wisdom of an older more experienced Christian, but that is exactly why we want to complete this study. God just might be calling you to be that person for someone else, loved ones! Pray about that today, won't you?

Day 5

Well, well. We've certainly had a busy week learning about mentors in the Bible. There are so many others, but certainly not enough room to share them all.

I hope, though, God's Word has established some thoughts in our minds about how important it is to have that accountability and guidance. This was exactly the point Paul was trying to make in the following verses.

Please read with me Romans 12:4-5 and 1 Corinthians 12:12-27. What do these verses say to us as Christians regarding the body of Christ?

_____

_____

_____

_____

Dear friends, each one of us has a job manufactured and designed especially for us! God has gifted every last one of His children with something that can be used for His work and His glory. One of the most important things women can do for those within the body is encourage and nurture other women who are needing a shoulder to lean on.

Obviously, not all of us are going to have the same gifts, yet through the Holy Spirit's prompting, we can make ourselves available to love those around us in such a way that lives are changed and spirits renewed.

31

You know, prayer is key in our walk with Christ.

In the next few blanks jot down the gift(s) He has given you. Next, pray and ask Him to develop in you a heart for others and compassion to make you aware of needs in the lives of other women. Ask Him to put into practice the characteristics we've learned as we have journeyed together this week, and to open opportunity to use your gift(s) in service to Him.

_____

_____

_____

_____

_____

_____

_____

_____

_____

_____

_____

He's going to bless you this week...I just know it!

Week 2
Reverence and Awe

Day 1

Glad to be back with you today! Walk with me as we look at mentors and the influence they can have on another's life.

As we spent the first week looking at examples of godly mentor/mentee relationships, now we are going to break down exactly what it means to be a mentor and what characteristics are found in this position.

I have two different Bibles I look into when trying to find the true meaning of a particular scripture. The one that gives me the most help is my Amplified Bible, which takes a particular verse and clarifies the English text by using more of the original Greek and Hebrew meanings. When I looked up our focal passage, Titus 2:3-5, this is what I found in verse 3a:

Bid the older women similarly to be reverent and devout in their deportment as becomes those engaged in sacred service...

Alright ladies, let's break this down. According to Webster's Dictionary, reverent means to be "holy" or to "show respect" for; devout means to be "passionately religious"; and deportment means one's "conduct". In this little sentence, God says a lot to us women. What I find most interesting, though, is at the end of the sentence where we see the words "sacred service". Paul is describing the role of the older woman and calls her service to God as sacred. For the most part, do we truly see our lives and work as sacred? Let's take a look back into scripture to find out who this God we serve really is and why our roles are so special and set apart.

In your Bibles, look up the following scriptures and state what the main theme is in each.

◆**Psalm 77:13**_____

◆**Psalm 99:3**_____

◆**Psalm 99:5**_____

◆**Psalm 99:9**_____

Okay, I hope you caught the pattern. There are a ton of references all throughout the Bible about God's holiness, but these are a few of my favorites. So now we know God is holy, but what exactly does that mean? God is set apart, uncreated, morally perfect, light, and sacred! Is this the God you are worshipping? My sisters, if you could only catch but a glimpse of our creator in Heaven, you would understand more fully His magnificence and awesomeness. We worship a God who compares to no other.

We know through the study of His Word that those who encountered God did not walk away unchanged! Moses encountered God on Mt. Sinai and thus had to veil his face because of the radiance that shown round about him. The

Israelites encountered God at the base of the mountain and in Exodus 20:18-19 scripture tells us that *"when the people saw the thunder and lightning and heard the trumpet and saw the mountain in smoke, they trembled with fear. They stayed at a distance and said to Moses, 'Speak to us yourself and we will listen. But do not have God speak to us or we will die.'"* Isaiah encountered God and stated in chapter 6 vs. 5, *"Woe to me! I cried. I am ruined! For I am a man of unclean lips, and I live among a people of unclean lips, and my eyes have seen the King, the Lord Almighty."* People who encounter God are definitely changed!

In our look at the above scripture in Titus, we see that older women are to be changed...be different than the world. At this point in their lives, they should be walking with God daily and should be exemplifying the very qualities of God. Not only that, but they should hold their position in the Lord as **sacred**! Boy, doesn't that give us a new outlook on our role as women in God's kingdom!! Makes you feel kind of special, doesn't it?! We are to have reverence and awe of God and who He is. Likewise, we are to exemplify these characteristics in our very thoughts, actions, and words that they may rub off so to speak, on those around us. Let me shoot straight from the hip for a moment...a woman who feels God is calling her to a mentoring position should absolutely be grounded in God's Word and be involved in a thriving prayer life with her creator daily. If we can provide nourishment for our bodies each and every day, we can certainly provide sustaining spiritual food that is desperately needed. Remember, girls, *the body is temporary, but the soul is eternal.*

We'll stop there for today. Tomorrow we will continue on and look at the last part of verse 3. Until then...

Day 2

"...not slanderers or slaves to drink. They are to give good counsel and be teachers of what is right and noble."

Alright ladies, are you thinking what I am thinking? How often have we received a phone call or began an innocent conversation with someone, to very quickly find ourselves in a dialect that is displeasing to God and unwholesome?

Ephesians 4: 29-32 reminds us *"Do not let any unwholesome talk come out of your mouths, but only what is helpful for building others up according to their needs, that it may benefit those who listen. And do not grieve the Holy Spirit of God, with whom you were sealed for the day of redemption. Get rid of all bitterness, rage and anger, brawling and slander, along with every form of malice. Be kind and compassionate to one another, forgiving each other, just as in Christ God forgave you."*

How can what you say affect your testimony to non-Christians and those who are lesser in the faith?

_____

_____

_____

_____

_____

_____

How can bitterness, rage, anger, etc., affect your relationship with Christ?

_____

_____

_____

_____

_____

_____

As the verses remind us, what we say and/or harbor in our hearts can affect our testimonies. It's always good to remember that *words are like choice fruits, they must be handled carefully or they will bruise.*

I'm sure we can all think of a time when someone's words bruised us. God's Word is clear, though. We are to build up, not tear down with the things we say.

Let's move on.

The last part of the verse mentions that the Titus 2 woman is not to be a slave to drink and that she should offer good counsel and teach what is noble and true. Let me ask you; are you a slave to something or someone? For example, we know that alcohol is a drug and can be addictive. It is a mind-altering substance. If you have your mind altered in some way, you are definitely not thinking clearly and especially not thinking clear enough to offer wise counsel. This can also apply to a person, place or thing. Whatever you have allowed to gain control over you, has become an idol, and has altered your thinking. In essence, you have become a slave to your passions. You have allowed it to misdirect your focus and take your eyes off Jesus Christ and place them on the object of your affections. Just imagine for a moment going to a pastor for words of wisdom and godly counsel. The funny thing is, the pastor is not truly listening to you and does not have the faintest idea on how to guide you because he has directed his focus elsewhere!

This leads us to our next point —good counsel and teaching. We will hit on that tomorrow, so be ready!

Day 3

Wise Counsel/Sound Teaching

Growing up, my mother was always there waiting to offer advice when I needed it. Of course, as a teenager and young adult, I did not always want to hear what she had to say, for I thought I knew everything! As I have grown older and have become a mother myself, I am still not always ready to hear what she has to say, but most of the time, her more experienced wisdom offers counsel that is wise and thoroughly prayed out. I have discovered that though it may be painful at the time, because of her love and concern for me, her words are always honest and true.

As a mentor, our words to those we counsel should always be out of love and concern for that person, a deep humility that can only be obtained through a relationship with Jesus Christ, and most of all, guided by our loving heavenly Father who knows each of us better than we could ever know ourselves.

Read the following passages:

Proverbs 2:6; Proverbs 11:2; Proverbs 16:18

According to the first verse, who gives wisdom? What is the biggest enemy that can get in the way of our counsel to someone who is truly seeking help and encouragement?

_____

_____

_____

_____

_____

_____

_____

Pride can be one of our biggest enemies in our spiritual life. Especially true when we are counseling someone, leading a group, teaching or mentoring. We must always guard our hearts and minds so that we do not allow ourselves to become "puffed up".

1 Corinthians 8:1-3 says, "...We know that we all possess knowledge. Knowledge puffs up, but love builds up. The man who thinks he knows something does not yet know as he ought to know. But the man who loves God is known by God." When we are in a leadership position, it is very easy to allow pride to

enter our hearts. Be ever so cautious and allow God's Word and direction through the Holy Spirit be our guiding forces instead of our head "knowledge".

Ladies, always remember that ministry is never about us. It is totally and utterly about God. Everything you do should be for His glory and His alone. When it gets to be about you, it's time to step down and allow God to step in.

Let's take a look at some godly counsel in the Bible.

Read 1 Samuel 12:19-25. What did the Israelites ask Samuel to do for them?

_____

_____

_____

_____

What are some things Samuel told the Israelite people to do. What would happen if they did not heed this counsel?

_____

_____

_____

_____

_____

The Israelites realized that they had sinned against God and that He was ready and able to bring punishment upon His people for their disobedience. They cried out to Samuel for prayer and counsel on their behalf. God spoke through Samuel's words to this degenerate people and warned them to not turn away from the Lord, but to serve Him with all their heart. He encouraged them to be faithful, to fear the Lord and to consider what great things He had done for them. Hmmm. Sounds like wise counsel!

Have you ever been in a situation which you knew at the time was wrong, but had gotten so swept in that you needed help getting out? Maybe you have asked for prayer from someone you recognize as spiritually "in-tune" with the Lord, and they have given you similar counsel. Be wise! Fear the Lord and turn from your sin. Follow God's Word and the Holy Spirit's guidance. As for those who counsel, you can never go wrong with His guidance and leadership. God's Word brings forth life and understanding. It's a tool to be utilized. Be sure and use it, but handle it with care!

God's Word challenges us to be teachers. Let me tell you girls, teaching is a gift from the Lord and shouldn't be taken lightly. However, we are all teachers in some way or another. I'm sure each one of us can think of a teacher in our past that definitely made a difference in our lives by challenging our thinking and spurring us on to excellence. I certainly have been blessed by teachers throughout the years who have inspired me to always put my best foot forward.

Being a shy little girl growing up, I struggled with insecurities and fears of failure in many different areas. It seemed that I just needed that extra little boost of attention and love to help me along on my journey through life's lessons. I have had teachers who encouraged my creative side, teachers who encouraged my intellectual side, but most of all, it was the ones who taught me life lessons and truths about God which made the most lasting impression on me.

Can you think of a time or a special teacher which left a lasting impression on you? If so, share those thoughts here.

_____

_____

_____

_____

_____

_____

_____

_____

_____

_____

_____

_____

As we end today's lesson, stop and pray for a teacher who has made a difference in your life or one you know who just needs a little encouragement.

Day 4

Welcome back!

Continuing on, in Titus 2, vs. 3b and 4, older women are exhorted to teach younger women *"what is right and noble"* in order that they will be *"sane and sober of mind (temperate, disciplined) and to love their husbands and their children."* Now you would think that young women in the church would automatically understand discipline and her role as wife and mother, right? Not exactly. In today's culture, the church is becoming the dumping ground for all the broken pieces of people's lives. Girls and boys are dropped off by parents who just need them out of their hair for awhile. Many teenagers and women are attending in order to fit in somewhere, all the while not really understanding the God they are worshiping. There are broken lives and deep wounds which have to be dealt with. Many of the women in our churches today were not brought up with godly parents and have no example of how a woman is to carry herself. I have heard all too many times criticism from older women on younger women who are just "obnoxious". What we have to realize here, is that many of these "obnoxious" women have not had a role model and do not know or understand God's Word. More than likely, they may not even know God Himself! It takes great love, patience, and prayer on our part to take them under our wing and teach them the truths of God. Through His Word and the power of the Holy Spirit, we can see great transformation if we allow Him to work!

Read John 13:15 & 1 Timothy 4:12: What kind of teacher/servant are we called to be?

_____

_____

_____

_____

_____

_____

Read 2 Timothy 3:1-7: What are some things that we see today in society that can apply to women within the church? *These things are characteristics that all women need to be cautious of!

_____

_____

_____

_____

_____

_____

_____

_____

As we touched on above, the last part of the verse mentions that the older women must train the younger women to love their husbands and children. What an odd statement don't you think? Not really. As you look around at church congregations throughout this country, it is hard to comprehend the number of divorces among so-called "Christians". Families are being torn apart left and right all at the hand of the one who destroys. The good news is God has placed examples in our midst whose marriages have been a blessing, not a burden. These are women who have learned to rely on Him through the difficult times and have taken seriously their charge to love, honor and obey. Younger women can learn from these dear ladies. They can be encouraged to love their husbands and honor him as Christ has called them to do. Younger women can learn from an example of a godly marriage and thus be challenged to live out the principles of a godly wife.

Now to the issue of mothers and children, let's just face it: younger mothers desperately need guidance when it comes to rearing children. Child rearing can be a very exhausting and taxing opportunity. These moms need the wisdom and godly counsel of older women who have gone through and experienced some of the difficulties they are faced with. They need to realize that they are not the only ones who are experiencing hardships or challenges and that there is light at the end of the tunnel. As a mother, many times I have just needed to be reminded that I will have clean carpets and hole-less walls someday after the children move out! Again, the mentoring woman can provide encouragement and guidance that is so desperately needed in younger women today.

Turn in your Bibles to Proverbs 31, starting with vs. 10 through 31. As you read the following verses, list some of the qualities of a godly wife/mother:

_____

_____

_____

_____

_____

_____

_____

_____

_____

_____

As you read these verses, were you amazed, discouraged or encouraged by them? I think we must all take a step back and see what the deeper meaning to this passage says to us. First of all, we are to be women of action! The days of sitting on the sofa eating bon bons is long gone, ladies (if they were ever here, no one told me!). We are to faithfully and honestly provide for our families. Whether you work outside the home or you work within, you must do it as "working for the Lord".

Society today is very time-consumed. We rush to work and home again, rush to the store, to school plays, church activities, sports games, etc. In the middle of all the chaos, we balance the cell phone, email and checkbook while we stir the pot with the available hand. There are runny noses to wipe, doctors to visit and, yes, if we have time, husbands to attend to.

If we are completely honest with ourselves, there are things that must be done in order to survive, and then there are things that are needless extras.

Regardless, we are women of action. What we must not lose sight of, though, in the midst of our hustle and bustle is our significance in Christ!

Being very honest, what are some areas in your life whether you are younger or older, that need improvement? Has God spoken to your heart about issues you haven't quite resolved with Him? Write them here and then pray that He will help you overcome them and become the godly woman He knows you can be.

_____

_____

_____

_____

_____

_____

_____

Day 5

"Therefore, my dear brothers, stand firm. Let nothing move you. Always give yourselves fully to the work of the Lord, because you know that your labor in the Lord is not in vain." 1 Corinthians 15:58

I have this scripture typed up and hanging on my filing cabinet at work. It is a great reminder to me to keep on pluggin'. In being a godly woman and a mentor to others, we need to remember that our labor is not in vain. Each word of wisdom that you speak, encouraging note that you send, and comforting visit that you make, will glorify our heavenly Father and build an eternal reward that will some day be cast at the feet of Jesus. You will probably never know the impact you have on one's life here on earth. Sisters, we have marching orders and we need to begin the march!

Please read Galatians 6:9-10. What do these scriptures remind us of?

_____

_____

_____

_____

_____

_____

_____

When I ask my children to do something, especially if I know it is something they could easily make a mistake on, I carefully leave step by step instructions. My goal is to make it clear to them exactly what I expect them to do. So this is with God's Word. He has graciously laid out the plan of expectation. No, we will not have it all together in a week or so. This will take a lifetime of His constant guidance and provision.

In Psalm 40:5, the writer David writes *"Many, O Lord my God, are the wonders you have done. The things you planned for us no on can recount to you; were I to speak and tell of them, they would be too many to declare."* In verse 8 it states *"I desire to do your will, O my God; your law is within my heart."* Let me just ask you...has God done wonders for you? Can you truly say that you desire to do His will? As a woman and as a mentor/mentee, our prayer should be to desire His will for our life and marvel at His wonders. The exciting thing is when you can share that with someone else who understands!

Marvel at Him today, loved ones. Pray that He will make you into a woman of grace and beauty.

See you next week.

Week 3

Feathers of Friendship

Day 1

Well, it is my sincere hope and prayer that you and your study group have walked away from this look at mentoring with more than what you came in with. If not, then at least we had fun gathering together, right?!

You know, mentoring is so needed within our churches and women's ministry groups, but it has been my experience that we are doing a lot of talking about it, with little action. This week we are going to focus on the actual task itself—mentoring—and how to get started. Let's begin by looking at the first and most important step in a mentoring program...**Prayer.**

Prayer is critical when it comes to the Lord's work. First, we must determine if it is even His will for us to be a mentor at this particular time in our lives. Secondly, we need to begin praying for ourselves that He will use us to be a blessing to someone who is desperately in need of a guide and a friend. I'm assuming it's a given that we should furthermore be praying for our mentee, even if we don't know yet who they are.

The Psalmist David writes in Psalm 40:8, *"I desire to do your will, O my God; your law is within my heart."*

Yes, *daily* we are called to be living examples of godly women to those around us, but not every woman is ready to take on mentoring until they themselves have grown spiritually and matured in the faith. As I pointed out in last week's lesson, a mentor *must* have a daily quiet time with Bible study and prayer. We certainly cannot expect to offer any pearls of wisdom if we ourselves haven't opened the oysters from our heavenly Father.

Look up the following scriptures: Deuteronomy 32:47, Psalm 42:1-2, Joshua 1:8, 2 Timothy 3:16-17. How are we to feel about our quiet time with God and His Word, and why is it vital that we have a daily quiet time?

Now read Psalm 5:3 and Mark 1:35. What is the best time to have your quiet time?

_____

_____

_____

_____

_____

_____

_____

Let me just say that there is no law that says you must have your quiet time in the morning hours, but what better way to begin your day than spending time fellowshipping with the Father and allowing Him to speak to you!

My dear friends, each and every morning is a cherished moment for me when I grab my glass of chocolate milk and sit down in my old beat up chair with Bible in hand (no, I don't drink coffee, I've always drummed to a different beat!) How awesome it is to be in Almighty God's presence lifting up my praises to Him and listening for that still, small voice. Wow! Just thinking about it gives me goose bumps! Let me challenge you today to pick that time when you can pull yourself away from the every day routine, and spend some alone time with God. You won't regret it...I promise!

Read 1 Timothy 2:1-4. According to Paul, what types of things should be offered up in prayer?

_____

_____

_____

_____

Yes, ladies, we are to make our requests known to God, yet we are also told to pray prayers of intercession and thanksgiving for the things God has so richly given us. We are to pray for those in authority over us and those who persecute us. Prayer is powerful and effective in our daily walk, and vital in a mentoring relationship.

Let's stop for today, but take a few moments to pray that God will give you a passion for Him, His Word, and His plan to use you in someone's life.

Write a simple prayer in the space below for your mentee. Be sure and remember them each day when you have your quiet time. You will definitely begin to see God at work in their life.

_____

_____

_____

_____

_____

_____

Day 2

Welcome back. Yesterday, our focus was on prayer, and so it should be. Today, however, we will look at casting our net to find those who might be interested in both mentoring and being mentored.

Let me just start by saying that God is going to open your eyes to women within the church who need to be involved in this program. But, it has been my experience that not everyone will stand up and shout when the subject of mentoring is brought up. Those special ladies may just need a little Christian prodding! Case in point, when I first heard about mentoring, I imagined this long, arduous task of listening to someone's problems day in and day out for years and years. Ugh! Let me just tell you that mentoring has been the most rewarding opportunity that I have been given in women's ministry. I have developed strong friendships which I deeply cherish and have learned more from those I have mentored than they could ever have learned from me!

Turn with me and quickly skim through Matthew 4:18-22, Luke 5:1-11, and John 1:43-51. How did Jesus approach Peter and the other disciples about following him? What applications can you make from his example as you seek out those for a mentoring ministry?

_____

_____

_____

_____

_____

_____

_____

_____

_____

_____

_____

I hope you got something out of these passages. What they say to me is this. First, Jesus *chose* his disciples. He didn't put a flier in the bulletin at First Tabernacle Church of Jerusalem, which read something to the effect of "Looking for a few good men to fill twelve Disciple positions. Please see man in long, flowing robe named Jesus Christ for submission of application." No! He sought them out personally and told them to follow Him. He understood their heart. After observing them for awhile, he chose those who would ultimately sacrifice everything for God. We know from scripture that all but one of the disciples had a willing spirit and a servant's heart, which led to great ministries through the power of the Holy Spirit.

Now, granted, He did have a little more pull than you or I will have, and we probably need to ask and not tell someone about mentoring. Nevertheless, asking the right people is key. In John 17:6, Jesus says, *"I have revealed you to those whom you gave me out of the world. They were yours; you gave them to me and they have obeyed your word."* (emphasis added) Even Jesus, had chosen those whom His Father had revealed to Him. He didn't haphazardly pick and choose just anyone. As we seek women out for this special program, choose wisely and carefully those whom God reveals to you through prayer.

Next, we see that he chose men who were willing to get out of the boat. If you are beginning a mentoring program, or maybe feeling the call to mentor, then you will definitely have to get out of the boat! A mentoring ministry takes time, effort and a passion for helping someone else. Mentors must be willing to leave the security of their vessel at times and immerse themselves in the deep with their catch.

You or someone you have chosen to be a mentor must be willing to develop a close friendship with those they are mentoring. This takes time. You know, my mother always told me, "If there's something worth doing, it's worth doing right." I know now how true that statement really is. I have been mentored for a couple of years by our dear pastor. I'm sure that he has absolutely wanted to pull out his hair at times with my endless questions and chattering. As he has so patiently taught me through the Word and through wisdom of age, I have learned lessons that I will never forget. God's Word sticks to me like never before. The passion for reading and learning and wanting to grow spiritually has come from someone who has learned it himself through hours of study and preparation with God. This love of the scriptures and lifestyle of surrendering all to Him is exactly what mentoring should be about. For when you have God at the center of your life, everything will fall into place. Marriages, child rearing, jobs, household duties, relationships, etc., will be radically changed when your life is focused on Him and you are spending quality time at His feet. The disciples realized it, and their lives were forever altered!

Pray right now that God will divinely arrange a mentoring relationship in your life if you do not already have one, and that through this experience, both of you will grow and deepen your relationship with Him.

See you tomorrow!

Day 3

Welcome back. You know, our time together is almost coming to a close. Only a few more lessons, and then you will be on your way to a rewarding experience as you seek out a mentoring relationship.

Today we are going to focus on finding Biblical resources that mentor/mentees can use to help in their spiritual walk and their specific roles. As I'm sure you can imagine, our first and foremost resource is the Holy Bible.

Look up Hebrews 4:12. What does this verse say about God's Word?

_____

_____

_____

_____

_____

_____

Let's face it, scripture is completely relevant to any problem, care or concern which may arise in a mentoring relationship. It should always be used as a tool for guidance and direction in finding God's will in any given situation. His Word is living and active and consistently brings health to the soul and nourishment to one's bones! The Bible has been so intricately woven together that there is not one thing a man or woman may experience that God hasn't already provided an answer for in His scripture.

I have often found that when I am counseling someone, it is in those vital moments that I need a quick reference in locating meaningful verses in God's Word. If you are like me, you may remember the verse but cannot, at that particular moment, find it. Our youth pastor pointed me to a handy little book which I keep on my desk entitled, <u>Quick Scripture Reference for Counseling Women</u>, by Patricia Miller. You can find it at <u>www.bakerbooks.com</u>.

This particular reference book covers topics such as abortion, abuse, anger, bitterness, divorce, faith, gossip, illness, laziness, quiet time, rape, singleness, unsaved spouses, and many others. It is definitely a handy little tool when dealing with these delicate situations.

Another great resource is through RBC Ministries. RBC offers many little booklets that touch on numerous topics. In our church, we purchase hundreds of these tiny gems to have available for those struggling with certain areas, or just as a reference for those who may want to know more of what the Bible says about a particular subject. Topics such as divorce and remarriage, unfaithfulness, illness, wayward children, depression, the occult, death, etc., as well as quick studies on books of the Bible may be found at www.rbc.net.

As leaders of women's groups and mentoring programs, it is always incredibly important to seek out and find solid, Biblical reference materials when mentoring or counseling someone through delicate situations.

Today anyone can choose from numerous so called "Christian" help books, but when comparing it to God's Word, can clearly see that these are nothing more than self-promoting, "health, wealth and prosperity" fluff. Be ever so careful what you allow to be put into your minds. This is definitely where you will need to pray for a spirit of discernment.

Pray that God will protect your mind and heart as you seek to find not only scripture that will guide and direct you, but other godly materials to help you and your mentee on your journey together.

Until tomorrow, have a great day!

Day 4

"By perseverance the snail reached the ark." – C.H. Spurgeon

Well ladies, have we reached the ark yet? We're almost there! The light is at the end of the tunnel. The flower is almost ready to bloom. Are you excited? I know I am. Within the past couple of weeks, God has called me into yet another great opportunity. I have been asked to be the mentor for our local MOPS group (Mothers of Preschoolers). What a wild ride it is to be in the center of God's will! I'm not sure about you, but there are times I have had to step back and look at myself and say, "God, are you sure you are talking to me?" Yes, dear ones, He's talking to you! It's time to step out in faith and begin that great journey of mentoring. Perseverance is key! Once you start this, there will be no turning back. You must stay firm and move forward.

Deuteronomy 1:6-7 says, *"The Lord our God said to us at Horeb, 'You have stayed long enough at this mountain. Break camp and advance into the hill country of the Amorites; go to all the neighboring peoples in the Arabah, in the mountains, in the western foothills, in the Negev and along the coast, to the land of the Canaanites and to Lebanon, as far as the great river, the Euphrates.'"*

Let me just say, the Lord is telling us to break camp. We've stayed way too long and it is now time to advance! There are people—hurting, needy people out there—who are longing for God's truth and love to penetrate their hearts. We are His hands and feet and it is time we begin doing His work.

You may be thinking, "Well, I have all this new knowledge about what a mentor is and her duties as that guiding encourager, but what are some things I can do to begin that relationship?" Glad you asked!

Conversation is key to building any successful relationship. One fun way of kicking off your mentorship program is to throw a party! Every woman knows that food and fun equal lasting friendships. When you can get together and just let your hair down, bonds begin to bud and heart doors open. Once the first moments of awkwardness subside, true camaraderie and oneness can begin. I've seen God take all types, sizes and backgrounds of women and bring them not only into a relationship with Him, but with each other because of His son Jesus Christ and the common bond they share. What an exciting and rewarding moment that can be!

Before your party or kickoff event for your mentoring program, you will want to have each woman—mentor and mentee alike—fill out an informational survey sheet. This will reveal her interests, goals, and weaknesses, but more importantly, give her an opportunity to share why she wants to be part of a mentoring program and what areas in her life she would like to be challenged in. Also, what better way to find out where she is spiritually! This may open up a whole new opportunity to either challenge her in her walk with Jesus or give the green light to witness to a lost soul whom, without Christ in her life, is on a road of destruction and despair. Make it your goal, loved one, to always put her relationship with Christ first and foremost. Encourage her to aim for a deeper relationship with Him through His Word and the challenges He sets before each of us.

As you plan your event, you will also want to include an activity that the friends can participate in together. What better way to get to know each other one on one and build a lasting friendship!

Scrapbooking is an activity that our church has adopted as

a monthly gathering for our mentors and mentees to do together. Let me just say, get a group of women together with pretty paper, stickers and pictures, and the fun will begin!

Another idea that women enjoy is breaking for coffee at the local fru fru coffee house. If you're like me, the form of pampering myself comes in a hot cup of mocha latte with extra whip cream, and maybe a giant chocolate chip cookie on the side! Am I punching anyone's buttons? Let's just face it, women love to get together and gab and what better way to build that friendship but face to face with a hot (or cold) cup of Joe!

After nailing down the finishing touches of the first meeting, then exhale and look forward to the great time you will have getting to know your mentee and the other women. As each "friend" arrives, pair her up with the mentor that has been chosen according to interests and need. A great idea to start off the fellowship time is to have each mentor share a brief testimony and acknowledge areas that they need encouragement in. It is good for mentees to realize that even their mentors need to grow and be challenged in areas of weakness. The Bible plainly states in Proverbs 27:17, *"As iron sharpens iron, so one man sharpens another."*

Ladies, this is what mentoring is all about…women needing one another to strengthen and sharpen the other. Mentoring is never one person having all the answers. A mentor needs no specialized training, just a heart for the Lord and a love for His people.

My prayer for you is that your group of women— whether

large or small, will be strengthened by these new relationships. Don't get discouraged if your mentoring group starts out small. Instead, focus on the new work that is being completed in the lives that are participating. If you can reach one woman who needed that extra bit of encouragement, or that young mom who is at her wits end, then praise the Lord! God is at work through you!

Before we end today, make a checklist of some things you will want to know about your mentee when you get together for the first few times. This will help you develop questions to ask and/or general dialogue when speaking with her.

_____

_____

_____

_____

_____

_____

_____

_____

Quote for the day: *"Many of you have put a period mark by your commitment. You need to erase that period and let God lead you further, now!"* - Waylon B. Moore, mentor

Day 5 - Final Thoughts

It is so exciting to start a new adventure, but even more so when the time is finally ripe to taste the fruits of your labor. It is my hope that through this study God has revealed Himself to you in a whole new light and has shown you the next steps to take with Him. As you and your mentee begin this new friendship, remember the three L's: Listen, Love and Learn.

First, listen more than you speak. James reminds us in his book, chapter 1, verse 19, *"My dear brothers, take note of this: Everyone should be quick to listen, slow to speak and slow to become angry..."* God blessed you with two lovely ears. Dear one, let them do their job! Your mentee, your children, your husband, or whomever depends on you regularly, needs to know you care. Listening is a big part of any relationship because it demonstrates our genuine care and concern for the other's needs, not just focusing on our own. Make it a practice today to concentrate on what people around you are talking about and truly listen. You might just learn something!

Second, the scriptures remind us that love covers a multitude of sins. Let us remember to love and encourage those we mentor. Ephesians 5:1-2 says, *"Be imitators of God, therefore, as dearly loved children and live a life of love, just as Christ loved us and gave himself up for us as a fragrant offering and sacrifice to God."* We should imitate Christ in all that we do. He knows that it is not natural for us as individuals to love everyone we come in contact with. Yet, through the Holy Spirit indwelling within us, we can have that supernatural love for those we mentor as well as others who may cross our path.

Third and finally, learn. You know, we are never too old to learn. If you were to take a quick survey of men and women used of God throughout the Bible, you would see that many were called into service late in life. These blessed individuals did not hang up their hat after time had taken its toll, but were willing to continue learning and living for the One who called them onward.

As a mentor, a mom, a wife, etc., there will be many times God will challenge you in areas you need to learn more. Realize that He is never done with us until we are removed from this life. Proverbs 1:5 and 7 says, *"Let the wise listen and add to their learning, and let the discerning get guidance. The fear of the Lord is the beginning of knowledge, but fools despise wisdom and discipline."* There may be times that we are wise to listen and learn from those we are mentoring. God can and will use other people to draw us back to the relationship we may have slipped away from. There have been several instances when in moments of weakness and the fleshly nature, I have reverted back to some of my old ways of thinking or ungodly attitudes. It is at those times, God has humbled me through some dear soul who was bold and brave enough to remind me of my shortcomings. It has been in those moments that I have learned the greatest lessons. Ladies, sometimes we have to swallow our pride, learn from our sinful downfalls, and walk away changed because of them. Thank God for times of learning!

As we close, my challenge to you as a mentor is to stay focused and complete the course. God has called you into this challenging position of mentoring, and for this you must continue on to completion. Don't let the cares of this world, the everyday chores and to-do lists keep you from spending that precious time with your mentee or those whom God has placed in your care for a season. Make it your priority today to make time for them and show them how valuable they are to you.

May God bless you on your new journey of mentoring.

For the Leader

I just want to begin by saying thank you! Thank you for having this passion for Women's Ministry and for following Christ's lead in reaching out to those who need to be touched by the hand of God. As you prepare for leading your group over the next several weeks and thereafter, I pray that you will be in much prayer for the group as a whole and for yourself as you lead out.

To begin this study, set aside a day or evening, whichever works better for your group of women, and reserve it on the church calendar. Depending on your group's size, you may also consider hosting a home study over the next several weeks. It seems that women find it comfortable and inviting when they can settle in on a nice, big sofa with a plate full of snacks!

Begin to publicize the study and ask women to pray about the possibility of mentoring. Talk to your Pastor and encourage him to openly address the importance and Biblical significance of the older women mentoring the younger. Enlist women who are already in a mentoring friendship or who have been mentored in the past, and have them share with the congregation or your women's group the difference it has made in their lives.

Each week that you meet, start off with an ice-breaker to get the group loosened up a bit. One that I have used in the past is to go around the room and have each woman make three statements about themselves, two being true and one being made-up. The rest of the group then must decide which one is the false statement. The women I have played this with seemed to have fun (maybe too much!), and have learned new things about each person.

Another great game is to give every one an index card and a pencil. Have them write things such as their favorite color, food, holiday, what their hobbies are, their greatest fear, and something no one else may know about them. Collect the cards and then take turns drawing one out and trying to guess who that person is. This is another way of getting to know everyone in a non-threatening manner.

After the ice-breaker, it is a good idea to have a quiet time where women who have something on their heart can share their prayer requests. One way is to assign each woman as she arrives a color, symbol (smiley face, sunshine, music note, flower...), number, etc. and then have her pair up with the woman who has the matching assignment. This way the two can share their requests with each other and not the whole group. You may just want to ask for requests and jot them down, then either offer a season of prayer (a time for those who are willing and comfortable to pray) or ask someone in advance if they would be comfortable to pray for the requests.

First Meeting

The first meeting of the study, you will want to hand out the study booklets if you haven't already done so. Explain to them how you would like to see God use this study in their lives and in yours. Remember, the enthusiasm you show for the study and for this mentoring program will make or break it. If you truly do not have a heart or passion for other women, then it will show and the other potential mentors will soon lose interest as well.

Hand each woman a piece of paper and a pencil, and make sure they have a Bible as reference. Have them start out by writing what "Mentor" means to them. Go around the room and ask for volunteers to describe what they wrote.

Next, brainstorm on a large piece of paper (that is visible to all) some things women face in today's world that we as Christ's body can help them through, and what type of help may be needed in each situation. *Note – make sure the women in your group understand that there will be things that may arise that require the help of a professional Christian Counselor, Doctor or Pastor in dealing with certain issues. Know your limits.

Example: **Challenges Women Face**

Loneliness

Discouragement

Discontentment

Helplessness

Anxiety/Stress

Solution

Friendship

Encouragement

Trust in Him to provide for Needs;Find contentment in Christ

Hopefulness in Him through Prayer

Trust and Faith in God alone

After this activity, invite the women to take out their Bibles and skim the following passages (I realize they're lengthy) and name characteristics they find in each of the mentoring relationships. You may want to write these names and passages up ahead of time and pass them out, or do as group activities.

Elijah & Elisha – 1 Kings 19:19-21; 2 Kings 2:1-15

Nathan the Prophet & David – 2 Samuel 7:1-3; 2 Sam.12:1-14

Mordecai & Esther – Esther 2:7-23; Esther 4:1-17

Jesus & Peter/the other disciples – John 13:1-17; John 14:1-4

After each characteristic and quality has been shared (i.e. loyalty, teachable spirit, accountability, protection, servant hood, compassion, etc.), introduce the study and encourage the women to take their Bible study books home completing each day's text and assignment. Close your discussion in prayer and lift up those who choose to be a part of this great adventure!

Second Meeting

After everyone has arrived, begin with an ice-breaker such as the following.

Ice-breaker example: Each woman is given a list of 5 to 10 traits that they must find in common with the people around them. Sample items could be: "Find someone that was born in the same month", "Someone who loves ice cream", or "Drives a blue car". Have the woman sign her name under the description when they are located. Only give them 5 or 10 minutes and see who gets the most signatures.

Now that the women in your group have had a chance to open up and have fun, it would be a good time to settle down and again focus on prayer and the reason they are there. At this time you can answer any questions they may have about the study and let them reflect on something which may have stuck out in their minds from what they read.

Pass out a piece of paper to each woman. Have her number down the page to three, leaving space between the numbers. Present a mirror and pass it around the group. Ask the women to look at themselves and describe what they see (Number 1). Next, have them write what they think God sees as He looks at them (Number 2). Finally, write what they see as they reflect or *look* at God (Number 3). Say to the women, "As you looked in the mirror, what did you see? Just a reflection, or did you see flaws and imperfections? Did you like what you saw?" (You can pause for answers, but they may or may not feel comfortable revealing personal information). Continue, "What does God see when He looks at you? Does He see a Christ-like example; a *reflective image,* or does He see someone who has a lot of growing to do?" Lastly, ask, "How do you view God? Is He a cosmic killjoy, someone who is just there, or is He holy and beyond description, and holding your life in the palm of His mighty hand?"

Assure the women that we all have areas that we need to grow in, even if we have walked with Christ for many years! No one ever reaches perfection or completion until he or she enters God's kingdom. There are going to be things we like and dislike about ourselves, but God can use our weaknesses and turn them into strengths. Our goal is to take our eyes off ourselves and focus on Christ who can transform us into usable vessels for Him.

Remind the ladies that as they go through this week's study, they will be exploring the true make-up of a mentor. What the Bible says about the characteristics we should have. Tell them that our lives should become a "reflection" of Christ. As we grow and mature in the faith, we will reflect more and more Christ-like qualities, which in turn can be used to help others, thus mentoring.

Ask the women if there is anything anyone would like to share, then close the group with prayer. Challenge them this week to get into God's Word and let it penetrate their hearts.

Third Meeting

Make sure as the women arrive, they receive a piece of hard candy (buy a mixed bag so that everyone gets a different piece). Tell them not to eat it, but to take their piece and place it in a bowl that you have sitting in a prominent part of the room. After everyone gets settled in say, "When you came in, you were given a piece of candy. Every piece is different, yet it all has the same purpose. As you placed your candy in the bowl, you see that it all got blended together. I would like each one of you to take out a piece of candy you like and enjoy it." (pass around the bowl) Explain that this represents ministering to women through mentoring. We all come with something to share. We all have the same purpose (we were created by God and for God), and we walk away with something that is enjoyable and long lasting (unless you crunch it!). Lead your ladies in a time of prayer and then go over any questions or comments they may have from the homework in week two.

Explain to them that this week they will focus on how to get started in mentoring. You will want to have them fill out an informational survey sheet at this time revealing why they would like to mentor or be mentored, what their interests are, hobbies, birthday and/or anniversary, and most importantly, where they are spiritually. As the women fill their forms out (make up ahead of time), play some soft music in the background that has to do with friendship. An example would be "Friends" by Michael W. Smith or "Does Anybody Hear Her" by Casting Crowns.

After you have collected the survey sheets, have someone turn to and read in their Bible, Ecclesiastes 4:9-12. Remind the group that this is exactly why they are going through this study. God has called them to help their sister up, strengthen her, and keep her warm through encouragement, love and friendship.

Close in prayer and challenge each woman to be thinking about ideas this week for their times together with their new friend.

Kickoff Night

This is the fun part! Choose a special evening for your kickoff night (can be day event). Make sure you have childcare available for those with small children. Decorate your room with a theme of your choosing such as a fiesta, luau, garden party, etc. Make sure that you have sorted your survey sheets and paired up the mentors with the mentees by interest, backgrounds, etc., and have assigned seats for them at the same table.

Welcome your guests as they arrive and help them find their seat. At each table make sure there are conversation starters to get the women talking. For example, you could have questions taped to leaves on potted flowers or written across their placemat. Questions like "What was your first car?" or "Describe your favorite vacation". Be creative and have fun. Your hard work will pay off!

Make sure you have planned out your evening. You may want to have the evening filled with something hands-on like scrapbooking, or choose more of a formal event such as a holiday tea. (Note, you will definitely need extra hands in the planning of these events.) Along with your agenda, you may want to either have a speaker come in or have time of testimonies from those women who have agreed to mentor.

The rest is up to you. Encourage your mentoring pairs to schedule at least one outing a month for the next six months so that the friendship can have time to develop. If your budget allows, it might be nice to have some type of journal or calendar at each place setting so that the women can have something to write down their "get together" dates.

Finally, take a deep breath as you leave your kick off event, knowing that you have done your best as a leader. Leave these relationships in the Lord's lap and pray that He will water them and help them bloom.

May God bless you on your journey and in your new friendships!

Completely His,

Kristi

Plan of Salvation

Dear Friend, I just want to take a moment to ask you about your eternal security. Each one of us is going to die some day. Do you know beyond the shadow of any doubt that if you were to leave this world today, that you would enter God's heavenly throne room and be at peace with Him, and live with Him forever? If you are unsure, then let me tell you what His Word says about God, eternity and how you too can share in His glorious salvation.

First of all, we are all sinners. We have all told a lie, stolen something, disobeyed our parents, lusted after someone or something else, taken the Lord's name and used it as a curse word, etc. We are human and live in a fallen, sinful world. This sin and all its ugliness separate us from a God who is morally perfect, righteous and holy. But, because of His great love and compassion on mankind, He sent His perfect, one and only Son to die in our place on the cross. Even if you or I had been the only sinner ever to walk this earth, Jesus would have left His heavenly home and taken upon Himself all the awful, ugly sin that each one of us carries around.

I'm sure you have heard or read the old familiar verse, John 3:16, *"For God so loved the world that he gave his one and only Son, that whoever believes in him shall not perish but have eternal life."*

Romans 6:23 says, *"For the wages of sin is death, but the gift of God is eternal life in Christ Jesus our Lord."*

The Bible also says, *"There is no one righteous, not even one; there is no one who understands, no one who seeks God. All have turned away; they have together become worthless; there is no one who does good, not even one."* Romans 3:10-12

And further still, *"...for all have sinned and fall short of the glory of God"* Romans 3:23.

The apostle Paul writes that *"...God demonstrates his own love for us in this: While we were still sinners, Christ died for us."* Romans 5:8

Jesus Christ knew that there was no other way to get to heaven and be with the Heavenly Father but through Him. He once said, *"I am the gate; whoever enters through me will be saved."* John 10:9

But what are we "saved" from? The Bible is clear that if we do not surrender our lives to Christ, then we are doomed to spend an eternity in Hell, forever separated from God in unending torment and agony.

In Matthew 8:12, Jesus says, *"But the subjects of the kingdom will be thrown outside, into the darkness, where there will be weeping and gnashing of teeth."*

He also told a story about a rich man who went to Hell saying, *"The rich man also died and was buried. In hell, where he was in torment, he looked up and saw Abraham far away, with Lazarus by his side. So he called to him, 'Father Abraham, have pity on me and send Lazarus to dip the tip of his finger in water and cool my tongue, because I am in agony in this fire.'"* Luke 16:22b-24

John the Baptist said (talking about Jesus) *"His winnowing fork is in his hand, and he will clear his threshing floor, gathering his wheat in to the barn and burning up the chaff with unquenchable fire."* Matthew 3:12

The good news is, is that if you are reading this then it is not too late! My friend, the Bible says in Romans 10:9-11, *"That if you confess with your mouth, 'Jesus is Lord' and believe in your heart that God raised him from the dead, you will be saved."*

But that's not all. You must turn from your life of self and allow God to be Lord of your life. That means following Him and His will for you. 2 Corinthians 5:15 states that *"He died for all, that those who live should no longer live for themselves but for him who died for them and was raised again."*

If you have just now accepted the Lord Jesus as your personal Lord and Savior, then you need to bow your head, close your eyes and tell Him what you've done and ask Him to be Lord of your life, cleansing you through and through. The next step is to begin reading your Bible and find a good, Bible-believing church to attend. Then, share what the Lord has done for you this day. Welcome to the kingdom!

Resources for Women

Recommended Websites

Christian Counseling & Educational Foundation
www.ccef.org
$1 booklets on subjects such as depression, anger,
marriage, self-control, OCD, ADD, etc.

RBC Ministries
www.rbc.net
Booklets on every topic imaginable

Walk Thru the Bible
www.walkthru.org
Monthly devotional booklets – Tapestry for Women

Timeless Texts
www.timelesstexts.com
Quick Scripture Reference for Counseling
& assorted pamphlets on various topics

Resources for Women

Recommended Reading

Faithful Women & Their Extraordinary God,
by Nöel Piper

Hinds' Feet on High Places,
by Hannah Hurnard

The Keys to Spiritual Growth – Unlocking the Riches
of God,
by John MacArthur

A Shepherd Looks at Psalm 23,
by Phillip Keller

Resources for Women

Recommended Bible Studies

<u>A Woman After God's Own Heart</u>,
by Elizabeth George (book and study)

<u>Living Beyond Yourself: Exploring the Fruit of the Spirit</u>,
by Beth Moore (study)

<u>Woman to Woman Mentoring</u>,
by Janet Thompson
(study which includes a handbook and profile card
for Mentors and Mentees)

<u>The Excellent Wife</u>,
by Martha Peace (book and study)

Order more copies of

Between Friends

Call toll free: 1-877-212-0933
Visit: www.crosshousepublishing.com
Email: crosshousepublishing@earthlink.net
FAX: 1-888-252-3022
Mail copy of form below to:
CrossHouse Publishing
P.O. Box 461592
Garland, Texas 75046

Number of copies desired _____

Multiply number of copies by $ 9.95

Sub-total _____

Please add $3 for postage and handling for first book and add
50-cents for each additional book in the order.

Shipping and handling$_____

Texas residents add 8.25% sales tax $_____

Total order $_____

Mark method of payment:

Check enclosed _____

Credit card # _____

exp. date_____ (Visa, MasterCard, Discover, American Express accepted)

Name _____

Address _____

City State, Zip _____

Phone _____ FAX _____

Email _____

LaVergne, TN USA
01 October 2009
159662LV00001B/29/A